Original title:
The Moon Made Me Do It

Copyright © 2025 Creative Arts Management OÜ
All rights reserved.

Author: Evan Hawthorne
ISBN HARDBACK: 978-1-80567-800-7
ISBN PAPERBACK: 978-1-80567-921-9

Lunar Lullabies

When shadows dance and giggles swell,
A twinkling light casts a funny spell.
I tripped on air, oh what a treat,
Who knew my feet could be so sweet?

With starlit whispers, I start to sway,
The night steals my socks, in a playful way.
A giggle breaks from the sleeping trees,
As the world spins round, I'm lost in glee.

Enigma of the Night Sky

Why does the night pull pranks so sly?
A twirl of fate as I walk awry.
Each twinkle winks like a cheeky child,
And soon enough, I'm hee-hawing wild.

A tussle with shadows, I can't resist,
They tickle my toes, I laugh and twist.
In this cosmic game, I spin and sway,
As the universe chuckles and leads me astray.

Chasing Eclipses

A shadow strolls by with a mischievous grin,
I follow its lead, like a dance in the wind.
With each silly stumble, I can't help but cheer,
For the night is alive with laughter and cheer.

The stars join the fun, they shimmer and shine,
As I'm caught in a jest, sipping moonlight wine.
Forget about worries, let's dance on the lawn,
For chasing bright shadows, I'll never yawn.

Dreams Wrapped in Silk

In slumber's embrace, I tumble and roll,
With dreams made of silk, they tickle my soul.
Each giggle escapes as I float through the night,
This whimsical ride makes my heart feel light.

A twinkling prankster, oh what a tease,
Bends reality, makes my mind freeze.
With laughter that echoes, the cosmos in play,
My trusty old pillow leads the way.

In the Wake of a Silver Trail

A glimmer on the path ahead,
I follow with a grin instead.
The shadows dance, a cheeky play,
As giggles chase the night away.

With mischief in the starry air,
I trip and tumble, unaware.
The night invites a silly plight,
And laughter fills the moonlit night.

Secrets in the Cooling Breeze

A whisper in the evening's tune,
Pushed by the pranks of jolly June.
The breeze suggests a cheeky dare,
To steal some pie from Grandma's lair.

Oh what a chase, a raucous sight,
With forks and laughter taking flight.
Secrets shared with the stars above,
In the cooling breeze, we fall in love.

Enchanted by the Night's Eye

The eye that winks, oh what a tease,
It makes me play with such great ease.
A dance of whimsy here and there,
As if the night just doesn't care.

I wear my socks upon my hands,
And skip around like silly bands.
When mischief strikes, I want to shout,
The night's enchantments make me pout.

Trickster of the Twilight Veil

In twilight's glow, my spirit soars,
With playful pranks behind closed doors.
A jester lost in starry schemes,
I jest and giggle at my dreams.

A hat upon a cat I place,
As it prances with a regal grace.
The night unfolds in fits of fun,
Where laughter dances, everyone!

Night's Silver Sorcery

Under the stars, I found my way,
Caught in a spark that led me astray.
Dance like a fool, I twirled with glee,
Blame it all on that bright shiny spree.

Whispers of mischief filled the night air,
Chasing the breeze without a care.
With giggles and grins, I took to flight,
Oh, the wild things I did in the moonlight!

Under the Glow of Enchantment

There's something about that silver shine,
Turns me around, makes me feel divine.
I steal a bite of forbidden pie,
And laugh when questioned, 'Who, me? Oh my!'

With fairy tales dancing in my head,
I hop on the roof and bounce on my bed.
While shadows giggle and join in the fun,
I just can't resist – oh, I'm always the one!

Shadows of a Distant Orb

Under a hat that's crooked and bold,
I spin silly stories that never get old.
With sock puppets prancing all around,
I crown myself king of this silly town.

Straws as swords in a noble quest,
I challenge the fridge for a midnight fest.
Laughter erupts with a mischievous call,
As I juggle my snacks and just hope not to fall!

Constellation of Recklessness

A wink from the night, I can't hold back,
I start to wander – wait, what's that crack?
With every step, my antics grow bolder,
Laughing like pirates, my shoulders grow colder.

I wear my pajamas as my proudest attire,
With ketchup for ink, I script my desire.
The critters all chuckle, the stars start to twinkle,
In this raucous revelry, my heart starts to crinkle!

Embracing the Night Scents

In shadows thick, I dance with glee,
A whiff of mischief calls to me.
With lingering laughs and cheeky grins,
My wild escapade tonight begins.

Whispers of night, they tickle my nose,
A cascade of scents, who knows where it goes?
From cookies baked to muffins sweet,
Temptation's recipe, oh, what a treat!

Lunar Whispers in the Dark

The night patrols with glimmering light,
Beckoning me to join the flight.
In jester's cap, I prance around,
With laughter echoing, a joyous sound.

Giggles ripple as I sway and spin,
Crafting wonders where chaos begins.
The secrets shared under the stars,
Guide my antics, woven with jars!

Starlit Temptations

Underneath the winking lights,
I plot a scheme to steal the nights.
With glimmering eyes and a heart so bold,
I take to the skies, let stories unfold.

A pie left cooling, I make a bend,
A nibble here, just 'round the end.
The laughter echoes, my heist is grand,
In a buttery trance, I take a stand!

Celestial Mischief

The stars conspire, their twinkling schemes,
To fill my head with wild daydreams.
With cheeky winks they lead the way,
To silly pranks that come out to play.

Moonbeams tickle, ignite the night,
I chase the shadows, in pure delight.
The fun unfolds, a childlike cheer,
In cosmic games, I have no fear.

Crescent Creeps and Midnight Leaps

Under the glow, I prance and sway,
Chasing shadows that dance and play.
A mischievous grin as I skip on the grass,
Wondering what trouble will come to pass.

In the woods, the owls hoot my name,
As I leap and twirl, playing my game.
Silly thoughts drift on this night,
Half-moon giggles make everything right.

Serenade to the Cosmic Muse

Starlit whispers float through the air,
Making me think of ideas to share.
Jesters of night, they tickle my mind,
To craft silly sonnets of the weirdest kind.

With the breeze as my partner, I strut and hum,
As goofy rhymes turn to rhythmically drum.
Laughter erupts from the giggly trees,
Their rustling leaves sing, "Just do as you please!"

Whirling in Lunar Light

Dizzy from dreaming, I twirl with delight,
Spinning around till I'm lost in the night.
No clue where I land, but I'm grinning wide,
As stars wink at me, they become my guide.

Frogs croak a tune and I join in the fun,
Pretending I'm dancing with everyone.
The silver glow casts shadows in jest,
A whimsical whirl that's simply the best!

Moonlit Lures and Midnight Fancies

With sparkly eyes, I creep through the gate,
Chasing the sounds of the night, oh great!
A secret soirée where silliness reigns,
As I slip on my shoes and go dance in the lanes.

From bouncy fairies to giggling ghosts,
This moonlit caper, oh how it boasts!
Twinkling adventures in every corner,
Where laughter erupts, turning frowns to shorter.

Enchanted Echoes in Midnight's Realm

In the still of night, I prance,
Frogs in tuxedos, join the dance.
Squirrels wear hats, oh what a sight,
Under silver beams, we take flight.

Whispers of shadows, secrets unfold,
A raccoon juggles, so brave, so bold.
With nighttime snacks, we share a feast,
Laughing and playing, never frequent least.

The garden gnomes raise their cups,
Toasting to mischief and giggling pups.
While shadows leap with joyous glee,
In this wild dream, I'm just so free.

As dawn approaches, we part ways,
With stories of laughter to fill our days.
But tonight I'll return, no need to fret,
For echoes of fun are not over yet.

Tugged by the Celestial Strings

Swaying like marionettes on a string,
While crickets chirp and fireflies sing.
Bouncing on clouds, we start to twirl,
In this crazy world, watch my world unfurl.

With giggles that echo through the dark,
We ride on owls that bark and spark.
A hedgehog winks, what a sight indeed,
In whimsical fun, we all take heed.

The stars above, they wink their eyes,
As we perform under velvet skies.
With antics galore and laughter's ring,
Our playful hearts dance, as we swing.

When morning comes, our laughs will fade,
But these funny tales will never jade.
For on this night, under twinkling bling,
We've felt the thrill of the celestial fling.

A Serenade to Starlit Yearnings

Beneath the stars, I strum my lute,
While puppies chase their bouncing boot.
Every note twirls through the night,
Bringing giggles and pure delight.

The owls hoot back, they know the tune,
While moths tango beneath the moon.
Each wisp of wind carries a jest,
In this serenade, we're truly blessed.

Oh listen close, a chorus begins,
As crickets weave in the silly spins.
My shadows dance with the giggling trees,
A night of laughter, a heartfelt tease.

When dawn peeks in with soft, warm light,
Our melodies fade, bidding goodnight.
But in sweet dreams, we'll parade once more,
In the starlit world we all adore.

Daring Adventures in Twinkling Shadows

In the midnight hours, mischief brews,
As kittens plot and puppy crews.
With capes made of leaves, we take our flight,
Adventurers bold, under the starlit night.

The fence becomes a castle wall,
Where giggles resonate, daring us all.
We joust with broomsticks, swords in hand,
In this whimsical world, we make our stand.

The shadows flicker, playing tag,
As my rubber ducky starts to brag.
To the end of the garden, we run so fast,
With laughter and silliness, we'll make it last.

When the sun awakes, we'll sigh with glee,
For these daring nights are our jubilee.
With stories to tell of all our fun woes,
In the thrilling shadows, anything goes.

Seduced by Phases of Desire

When the silver light starts to glow,
I dance in dreams, my heart in tow.
With laughter loud and mischief bright,
I trip over shadows in the night.

Whispers twist in the starry air,
Telling tales of a lover's snare.
I don my crown of wild flowers,
Underneath these hush-hush hours.

Full of giggles, I sway with glee,
Winking wisely at the trees.
Caught in this soft and silly trance,
I'll blame the sky for my wild dance.

Mischief Under Starry Covers

Beneath the quilt, the secrets creep,
While nocturnal giggles fill my sleep.
With every rustle and joyful sound,
I paint the night with fun profound.

A pillow fight under cosmic beams,
Where laughter bursts like sugar dreams.
Tossing stars like shiny beads,
In this chaos, the heart proceeds.

When blankets fall, the world is small,
I toss the rules, I toss them all.
Cozied up with mischief's tale,
The night is ours, we shan't derail.

Shadows of the Ethereal Watcher

Oh, to be watched by a glimmering eye,
As I trip and tumble, oh my, oh my!
The shadows chuckle, the night's a jester,
Playing tricks as my heart flutters.

Chasing dreams that slip and slide,
With each silly misstep I take in stride.
Those glowing orbs up there have fun,
Plotting chuckles while I run.

In their gaze, I lose my way,
Dancing like a fool, come what may.
With giggles echoing in moonlit air,
I might just do something beyond compare.

Navigating by Moonbeam

With a wink from the sky, it's time to roam,
Through the night, I've made my home.
The beams are my compass, shining bright,
Leading me to whimsy's delight.

In sneakers or slippers, I prance and play,
Chasing shadows that want to sway.
Each step is a joke made just for me,
Laughter dances, wild and free.

Oh, how easy it is to get waylaid,
Lost in the fun that the night has laid.
With a grin on my face, I glide and spin,
Thank you, dear stars, for this joyous sin.

Secrets Beneath the Stars

Whispers of laughter float in the breeze,
As shadows play tricks among the trees.
A giggle escapes as I trip on a root,
Stumbling through secrets, what's the dispute?

The night wears a cloak of glitter and glee,
Chasing the fireflies, oh how they flee!
Each twinkle a riddle, each dart a sign,
Led by the mischief of a light so divine.

With friends close beside and snacks at the ready,
We plot silly schemes, our humor's steady.
Moonlit adventures, a comedy spree,
Is it the night or just foolery?

In this world of magic and playful delight,
We dance in the glow, till the dawn takes flight.
Secrets are blooming, the laughter won't cease,
Under the stars, we find our release.

When Darkness Calls

A shadow unhinged from the safety of bed,
Whispers of fun run wild in my head.
As darkness encroaches, what shall I do?
Perhaps a mischief or two will ensue.

With a sneaky giggle, I tiptoe outside,
Finding new games that the night will provide.
From frogs in the pond to the stars' serenade,
Who knew my adventures would never fade?

Socks on my feet, a mask on my face,
I'm a ninja of giggles, in my own little space.
The night is my stage, the world my delight,
With shadows and silliness dancing in sight.

As morning arrives and the laughter subsides,
I creep back to slumber, where daydreams abide.
But tonight promises more, oh what a haul!
The antics shall flourish when darkness calls.

A Dance with the Nightlight

Oh, what a sight, my room's aglow,
With shadows that wiggle and giggle below.
I twirl around with my trusty sidekick,
A monster of dreams, who makes me laugh quick.

With each little step in this wild moonbeam,
I dance with delight, lost in a dream.
The floorboards can creak like an old rusty tune,
As I leap and I twirl in the light of the moon.

Lampshades and pillows become my best friends,
Twisting and turning till daylight descends.
Nightlight's my DJ, with beats soft and sweet,
Grooving with glee, on this whimsical street.

As dawn starts to creep, the fun starts to fade,
But tomorrow, I promise, will bring a parade.
For every sweet giggle and dance under light,
Is just a warm-up for next fun-filled night.

Light of the Enchanted Orb

In the backyard, with a shimmer and shine,
We gather 'round, sipping soda and lime.
There glows an orb with magic untold,
Its laughter like music, and stories unfold.

With each little flicker, we share silly tales,
Of unicorns surfing through candy cane trails.
The orb winks at us, it's part of the game,
Encouraging mischief, and who's to blame?

We toss marshmallows at friendly old trees,
While gathering wishes with soft summer breezes.
Guided by giggles, we dance like a swarm,
Under this beacon, the chaos is warm.

But when morning arrives, with yawns all around,
The orb bids us farewell without making a sound.
We grin at our secrets, tucked under our lips,
For adventures will follow on phantom-like trips.

Fantasies Cloaked in Midnight's Mystique

In shadows deep, I plotted schemes,
Twirling ideas like wobbly dreams.
A sparkly cape, a mask to wear,
Unruliness from a whispered dare.

Under soft glows, I pranced and leapt,
My pet goldfish, in secrets, crept.
With every chuckle and silly grin,
I felt the night just pull me in.

A sock puppet king, ruling my room,
We made a ruckus pretending to zoom.
My inner child led the charge that night,
In giggles and grins, I took to flight.

What mischief brewed beneath starry skies,
Held me captive in winks and sighs.
With mischief managed, the evening great,
I danced with the stars, oh what a fate!

The Dance of the Celestial Fireflies

Glowing dots in the garden sway,
Little lights leading me astray.
With each flicker, a giggle escapes,
As I chase their glow, in silly shapes.

A broomstick ride to the weeping willow,
Where laughter tickles my heart like a pillow.
In a tangle of legs and a burst of cheer,
I twirl with the fireflies, without any fear.

Topsy-turvy, I trip on my hat,
Stumbling forth, like a mischievous cat.
Their winks send me flying, oh what a scene,
In the dance of the night, I reign as queen.

With moon pies for shoes and laughter galore,
I prance in the night, never a bore.
As the stars giggle low, with a sway
I'll keep this folly for another day!

Encountering Whimsy in Soft Shadows

Midnight whispers tease my ears,
As puppets of mischief grow bold in their peers.
I tiptoe past whispers of dreams gone wild,
Under covers of night, I'm a mischievous child.

A shadowy figure, a hint of doubt,
Is it a creature or my giggle about?
Creaky floorboards join in the fun,
As my tales spin wild, like moonbeams run.

My pet cat, donned in a cape, quite the sight,
We formed a duo, embracing the night.
With swishes and twirls, oh what's the fuss?
We conquered sleep with joyful plus.

A prankster's glee, not a care in the world,
In the fabric of night, my laughter unfurled.
With whims and giggles, I lay down my head,
Dreaming of nonsense, till laughter is spread.

Evocations of Daring Under Starlight

Under twinkling lights, I made my plans,
To leap like a frog, in those wild spans.
A daring quest, I led my team,
With chuckles ready, like a silly dream.

Jellybeans in pockets, our secret loot,
Marching like soldiers, we'd dance and hoot.
Stupidity? Nay, it's a plan of delight,
In the glow of the stars, we danced through the night.

A pirate's hat atop my head,
Sailing through shadows, as our laughter spread.
The treasure? Just sweets, but heart so bold,
Our secret gang stories merrily told.

In daring escapades, we conquered the night,
With whims in our hearts, everything felt right.
And in jest we found our freedom grand,
With starlit giggles, we made our stand.

Visions Crafted in Night's Glow

In shadows where the mischief brews,
I danced with shadows in my shoes.
A twinkling wink, a playful tease,
I tripped on laughter, fell with ease.

The owls all hooted, eyes aglow,
As I tried tightrope on a low.
A twirl, a spin, a slip right near,
My neighbors now think I'm a seer!

A whisper told me to chase a cat,
I chased it round, imagine that!
Its furry tail became my guide,
In playful antics, we both glide.

With each bright star, a scheme was spun,
Who would've thought that night was fun?
I'll blame the glow for what I've done,
The night is over, with a laugh and pun.

Specters of the Darkened Dawn

In twilight's fun, I had a fling,
With brooms and hats, oh what a bling!
The ghostly guests, they laughed with glee,
As I tried to serve them ghostly tea.

The dawning light brought quite a fright,
Did I just swoon with ghouls all night?
They tapped their feet with eerie flair,
I offered snacks, they didn't care!

My cat now thinks she reigns supreme,
Atop my head, she's in my dream.
Just like the night, she's full of tricks,
With swats and paws, oh what a mix!

As morning creeps and shadows flee,
I'll laugh and wave to my ghostly spree.
With tickles, tricks, and giggles spun,
Who knew the dark could be such fun?

Raindrops on a Silver Tide

When silver drops come falling down,
I toss my hat and dance around.
Splashes loud, I giggle wide,
With puddles deep, I take a ride.

A duckling quacks, a splash it makes,
I join the fun, with silly shakes.
Each raindrop drips a silly song,
And in this dance, I can't be wrong!

With every leap, I laugh out loud,
The sky's my stage, I'm feeling proud.
Umbrellas twirl, they spin and sway,
While I just splash and laugh away.

The silver tide can't hold me back,
I'll chase the laughter, find my track.
Rain's a friend, we share the ride,
In every drop, there's joy inside.

Dreamscapes Stitched by Night's Hand

In vibrant dreams, I prance and play,
With silly twirls that lead the way.
The night's hand weaves a crafty scene,
Where laughter bounces, bright and keen.

A talking frog in a top hat waits,
He tells me tales of clumsy fates.
With every ribbit, giggles flare,
In dreamland fun, we share a chair.

I raced a snail, with zest and zeal,
He laughed so hard, I felt the squeal.
A parade of socks came marching by,
In rainbow stripes, oh how they fly!

As dawn arrives, my dreams retreat,
But echoes linger, oh so sweet.
I'll stitch more tales in twilight's grand,
With joyous hearts and laughter planned.

Nightfall's Engaging Embrace

In shadows deep where mischief stirs,
A wink from night, oh how it purrs.
With laughter bright, we trip and twirl,
As silly secrets start to swirl.

Beneath a blanket, stitched with glee,
We spin around like wild dervishes.
With every grin, the world feels light,
Chasing the stars, oh what a sight!

Whispers float on gentle breeze,
Dancing trails of giggles tease.
Each stumble brings a chuckled fright,
In this embrace of joyous night.

So grab your friends, and join the cheer,
For in this dark, there's nothing to fear.
The sky looks down with playful grace,
And we, the jesters, take our place.

Quickening the Heart Beneath the Stars

With starlit eyes and spirits bold,
A silly tale begins to unfold.
We trip on dreams, fall in delight,
Twinkling laughter fills the night.

The universe plays its tricks and games,
While we invent some goofy names.
From silly dances to silly tales,
Under the sun and moonlight gales.

Hearts race fast with every jest,
In cosmic chaos, we find our rest.
Spinning in circles, oh what a blast,
Making memories that forever last.

So raise a glass to stars above,
And celebrate this crazy love.
With every twinkle, we'll surely find,
Joy in the laughter left behind.

Whispers from the Silvered Sky

Under twinkling skies, we confide,
In giggles shared, and none to hide.
With shadows stretching far and wide,
A dance begins, let's take a ride.

Footsteps light, like whispers near,
Joking, laughing, without a fear.
Each clumsy move, a playful spin,
In this grand cosmic carnival we win.

Floating dreams like fluffy clouds,
Waving hello to friendly crowds.
In this bright sphere, joy shall reign,
As we proclaim our sweet refrain.

So let's embrace the giggly tone,
With starry hugs, we're never alone.
For in the sky's enchanting glow,
Laughter's the only way to go.

Dance of the Dappled Dreams

In dreams that dance, we take our flight,
With twirls and spins, we claim the night.
The world fades quick, we giggle loud,
In dappled glow, we're feeling proud.

With every misstep, laughter rings,
As joy explodes on flapping wings.
We bump and glide and sometimes fall,
Yet rise again, with goofy squeals and all.

With stars above, the stories weave,
Of silly things that we believe.
Caught in a whirl of charms so bright,
Our hearts leap high with pure delight.

So waltz with me, let's make some noise,
In this fantastic realm of joys.
For in the light of shimmering beams,
We find ourselves in dappled dreams.

Moonbeam Mischiefs Unveiled

In the night, I took a leap,
Socks on hands, not a sound to keep.
Dancing wildly, I lost my plate,
Waltzing with a rubber mate.

Under stars, I made a cake,
With frosting made of whipped-up shake.
Neighbors peeking from their doors,
Couldn't help but laugh and roar.

A raccoon joined, wearing a hat,
We held a party, imagine that!
Musical chairs with empty cans,
Even the cat joined our dance plans.

When morning broke, they called me mad,
But oh, the joy, it wasn't sad!
I'll cherish these absurd delights,
Until we dance again, moonlit nights.

Revelations Under Shimmering Lights

An owl hooted like a tease,
I snuck out, feeling the breeze.
With pizza slices in each hand,
I plotted pranks across the land.

Whispers floated in the air,
Balloons tied without a care.
A rubber chicken, what a sight,
Made everyone laugh with delight.

I painted spots on my own dog,
He strutted like a dancing frog.
Neighbors wondered what was wrong,
As we danced to a silly song.

With giggles echoing through the night,
I skipped around, feeling quite bright.
Not a soul could claim taboo,
Just laughter shared with a zany crew.

Echoes of Nocturnal Revelry

With whimsies wild, I took the lane,
Wearing mismatched shoes, pure insane.
A ghostly figure waved hello,
Turned out to be my shadow's show.

I painted my face with ice cream spritz,
Arguments with my pet goldfish.
In the yard, we threw a bash,
A garden gnome yelled: 'Let's clash!'

The sky giggled, lit with stars,
We played poker with candy bars.
My brother made a grand mistake,
Tried to bluff with a cupcake break.

When dawn appeared, it spilled the fun,
But memories sparkled like the sun.
In moonlit experiments, we grew,
Eccentric tales of our night anew.

Moonlit Gambols and Portentous Whirls

Sprung from bed with a strange intent,
To dance like nobody's ever spent.
A tutu made from old laundry stays,
I pranced around in a dazed haze.

Twinkle lights hung in the trees,
I swapped my coffee for bubble teas.
Slipping on slippers, flailing my arms,
A flash of whirls, surrounded by charms.

Silly shouts cracked the midnight calm,
As I serenaded a nearby palm.
With marshmallow swords, we dueled loud,
Reveling like a peculiar crowd.

As sunlight clawed the giggles down,
I wore my goofy victorious crown.
With echoes lingering in the lane,
I'll do it all again, oh how inane!

Whims of the Nocturnal Sphere

When shadows stretch and giggle wide,
I twirl like stars on a cosmic ride.
The night wraps me in playful schemes,
With laughter echoing in silver beams.

I dance with trees, the whispers cheer,
While owls hoot jokes we all can hear.
The breeze plays tricks, a gentle tease,
As fireflies wink with quirky ease.

I skip on clouds, forget my shoes,
And sing with crickets in silly blues.
Weightless in laughter, I spin around,
In the dark's embrace, pure joy is found.

As daylight fades, my mischief starts,
Creating chaos in moonlit arts.
The night's my partner, oh what a thrill,
In whimsical ways, I take my fill.

Lunar Dance of Secrets

Under the stars, a sly smile grows,
With every twinkle, my secret flows.
Skip through the night with playful schemes,
Chasing the shadows, fulfilling dreams.

I prance like a cat in pursuit of fun,
While the world sleeps, I'm just begun.
Beneath the moon's glow, so bold and sly,
I leap through the dark with a wink and a cry.

I tumble and giggle, a jester's delight,
Casting my wishes in the starry night.
Each secret shared, a giggle released,
The night's my stage, my joy's increased.

In shadows, I weave a tapestry bright,
Crafting my tales in bold strokes of light.
With laughter and joy, I ride through the air,
In this dance of the night, none can compare!

Tides of Enigmatic Dreams

With the tide's pull and a giddy twist,
I'm swept away in the night's brisk mist.
Each wave a giggle, each crest a cheer,
In this dreamlike realm, the fun is near.

I spot a seal dressed in a hat,
He juggles fish and says, "How bout that?"
The dolphins leap, and we all sway,
In splashes and grins, we dance and play.

A mischievous breeze lifts my hair high,
With whispers of dreams that flirt and fly.
Funny little creatures spin around,
In this drifty tide, pure joy is found.

In the moon's embrace, the night's alive,
With laughter and magic, I gladly dive.
Every wave a joke, every splash a cheer,
In tides of dreams, I have no fear!

In the Embrace of Nightfall

When evening spreads her velvet cloak,
I tiptoe out, bursting with joke and poke.
The stars are winking, the sky a swirl,
In the embrace of night, the antics unfurl.

With giggling grasshoppers playing games,
I dodge their leaps, while the firefly flames.
Each flicker a chuckle, a wink in the air,
As I bounce between laughter and playful care.

I climb up the moonbeams, oh what a sight!
Spinning and twirling, a raucous delight.
Together we tumble, my giggles collide,
In the embrace of night, I take a wild ride.

So here I remain, in this game I adore,
Chasing the shadows, forever wanting more.
The night whispers secrets, and I can't resist,
In silliness and joy, I happily persist.

Whispers from the Orb

Late night thoughts, they dance and sway,
I blame the glow for what I say.
Snack attacks, oh what a sight,
Chocolate bars by moonlight, quite the plight!

Giggles rise like tides at sea,
What was I thinking? Not sure, you see.
Dare I sing to silvery light?
The neighbors think I'm quite the fright!

Oh, cosmic friend, with your cheeky grin,
You lead me to mischief, I can't help but grin.
Midnight snacks and silly chats,
A starlit party where chaos hangs hats!

So here's my secret, just between us,
It's not my fault, it's the night's sweet fuss.
I'll toast to you, my shining muse,
For every whim that I might choose!

A Night's Command

Underneath your glowing stare,
I find myself in quite a scare!
With every wink, you pull me near,
"I'll dance," I say, "Oh dear, oh dear!"

Prancing like a goofy fool,
Who said the night was meant to cool?
Slippers on and socks askew,
Thanks to you, I've lost my view!

Midnight shenanigans take their toll,
I scratch my head, "Oh, what a goal!"
But laughing fits, they come in waves,
With every giggle, my spirit saves!

So here's to you, the night's decree,
You bring out the wild side in me!
I'll leave my worries 'til the dawn,
With every whim, I'm brightly drawn!

Celestial Callings

A twinkle here, a sparkle there,
I swear you called, but who knows where?
Lost in laughter, caught in light,
Jelly beans take flight tonight!

Your beams are sneaky, pulling strings,
In the silliness, the laughter sings.
Feet move fast, but brains in freeze,
With your playful tease, I take it with ease!

Around and round, the grand parade,
Silly faces in jokes we've made.
Each chuckle shines as bright as day,
It's you, dear friend, leading the way!

So let's keep spinning under your gaze,
With every glimmer, I'm set ablaze.
Oh, cosmic guide, with joy you spark,
In this feisty dance, we leave our mark!

The Allure of Dusk

When shadows stretch and laughter rolls,
You tease my heart, you sweet control.
Cool breezes whisper funny tales,
Of silly dances and epic fails!

You coax the mischief from my lips,
And send me off on wobbly trips.
Around the block and under trees,
I trip and stumble, yet feel the breeze!

With every glance, I dare to act,
A playful scheme, oh what a pact!
Banana peels and giggly friends,
We swirl with joy as laughter blends!

So here's to you, my nighttime muse,
Who crafts the chaos that I choose.
In every beam, I catch the jest,
You spark the joy that I love best!

Lunar Whispers in the Night

When shadows dance and giggle low,
I feel the pull, can't help but go.
The stars above wink with delight,
As mischief brews in the quiet night.

A pizza place calls my name,
With cheesy dreams, I stake my claim.
An empty fridge won't hold me back,
I'll feast till morning, that's the pact.

Neighbors peek through their window blinds,
As I prance about, my laughter blinds.
A juggling act with spoons and forks,
I'm a kitchen clown, the night is mine!

So, if you hear a raucous cheer,
Just know that I am lurking near.
With lunar whispers guiding me,
This playful trickster's antics are free!

Celestial Seduction

The night sky flirts with me tonight,
It sparkles and glows, oh what a sight!
A smooth distraction, silver glow,
I grin at the chaos I might bestow.

With ice cream cones and silly hats,
I challenge the wind, it giggles back.
A waltz with shadows, twirls of glee,
Join me in this cosmic spree!

Whispers of laughter fill the air,
As I sway like I don't have a care.
Dancing with clouds, I lose all sense,
In this fun frolic, I am immense!

So grab your shoes, come join my craze,
Under the stars, we'll dance ablaze.
With a wink and a nudge, let's have our fun,
Enjoy the night until we're done!

Under the Silver Sphere

The silver sphere whispers my name,
In its glow, I can't feel the shame.
With a twinkle in my eye so bright,
I venture forth into the night.

Bubble gum and neon lights,
Conspire together to launch my flights.
I spin, I twirl, a merry dance,
No reason here, just luck and chance!

With giggles echoing in the breeze,
I wear my quirks like autumn leaves.
A serenade of silly tunes,
Trickster spirit hums to the moons.

So come along and share my fare,
With laughter swirling like the air.
Under the sky, we'll laugh and play,
Embracing the whims of this wild array!

Nocturnal Temptations

When nighttime creeps and giggles rise,
I feel the pull, a sweet surprise.
Sneaky snacks in the cupboard call,
I stumble forth, will I stand tall?

With cookie crumbs stuck to my mouth,
I'm a playful fool from the north.
Twirling like a leaf in the breeze,
'Til I crash down with such quiet ease.

Neighbors whisper, 'What's that sound?'
As I leap and jump around.
A parade of clowns serving joy,
With laughter that no one can destroy.

So join my spree, don't be shy,
In the alchemy of the night sky.
With nocturnal charms, let's take a chance,
To live out loud in this crazy dance!

A Rhapsody of Celestial Chaos

Oh look at that pie up in the sky,
It winks at me, I can't deny.
I dance and twirl without a care,
My neighbors think I'm quite the rare.

With every step, I trip and fall,
The stars above just laugh and call.
A frolic fueled by a glowing sphere,
Who knew mischief would appear so near?

My cat joins in, he leaps with glee,
Chasing shadows, wild and free.
The garden gnomes, I swear they cheer,
As moonlit antics draw them near.

In rhapsody, we prance and sway,
As tangled thoughts come out to play.
A world awash in laughter's spell,
When nighttime mischief rings the bell.

Beneath the Silk of Night's Canvas

Under dark silk, a giggle hides,
With every glance, the humor rides.
A butterfly flutters in a bowler hat,
He tips it low while chasing a cat.

I juggle stars, or maybe just cones,
The ice cream melts, oh dear, my scone!
The owls hoot loud, they can't believe,
My clumsy dance, I can't retrieve.

Barefoot on grass, I spin around,
The crickets join as they make a sound.
Laughter echoes through the night,
While squirrels plot their next delight.

Slippery shoes and silly hats,
I laugh so much, I fall like that.
In the tapestry of dark and bright,
Fun takes flight on this crazy night.

Dreams Cast in Lunar Light

Caught in a trance by beams so bright,
I try to dance, but it's quite a fright.
My pajamas slip, I spin and twirl,
As laughter bubbles and starts to whirl.

A pizza slice floats up high,
With toppings dancing, oh my, oh my!
I reach for it, but magically it flies,
A prankster's feast beneath the skies.

While shadows giggle, I hum a tune,
The cookies grin, and less they croon.
My dreams take flight in airy delight,
In this bizarre, whimsical night.

Balloons appear with faces bright,
They bounce around, full of delight.
With every chuckle and silly feat,
The realm of dreams is oh so sweet.

Serpentine Paths of the Enigmatic Night

Down the winding paths I skip,
Dodging ducks on a lollipop trip.
The shadows stretch, making silly shapes,
A wizard's hat? Or maybe grapes?

Bouncing bunnies in polka dots,
Join my escapade with laughter's shots.
A road paved with marshmallow fluff,
Who would have thought this could be tough?

Talking trees whisper sweet, sweet rhymes,
But get it wrong, they throw sweet limes.
I dodge and laugh, they chase in jest,
On these funny paths, I am blessed.

With every turn, a giggle's found,
The quirky creatures dance around.
In a world where absurdities ignite,
Each step is taken in sheer delight.

Illuminated Desires

In the glow of night, I dance and prance,
With goofy moves, I take my chance.
Dreams of cookies fill my mind,
Blame it on the beams, my cravings unconfined.

Under silvery lights, I grab a snack,
A silly grin, there's no turning back.
Imagination soars, I'm a playful sprite,
Laughing in the shadows, oh what a sight!

With each twinkle bright, my antics unfold,
Like shadows of mischief, tales to be told.
I juggle the stars, a whimsical show,
In the land of dreams, my giggles flow.

So join me here, in this gleeful plight,
Where laughter and joy take playful flight.
With the night as my friend, we'll roam and spin,
In this delightful chaos, let the fun begin!

Gravity of the Night

As the sun dips low, my spirit's set free,
I trip over shadows, oh woe is me!
A clumsy ballet, a laughable sight,
Caught in the web of a whimsical night.

With stars as my audience, I take a bow,
Uncoordinated moves, I wonder how.
Gravity pulls, but I float like a dream,
In the laughter-filled air, nothing's as it seems.

Whispers of chaos echo through space,
Comets of chuckles, a shimmering race.
The glittering sky has me in its hold,
In the humor of night, I feel so bold!

With giggles for rockets, I soar to the heights,
Where the silly and laughter mix with the lights.
In this playful embrace, come join me tonight,
As we dance through the chaos, bathed in delight!

Moonlit Mischief

Under a blanket of velvet blue,
I plot my schemes with a mischievous crew.
Cookies and candy, they're calling my name,
With each silly idea, I play a new game.

Sneaking in shadows, we giggle and plot,
A heist of snacks, oh, we're thinking a lot!
I tumble and trip while wearing a grin,
In this delightful chaos, let the fun begin!

Laughter resounds as we dance through the dew,
Chasing the dreams that twinkle and skew.
With a wink and a nudge, we lift off the ground,
In a quirky ballet, we twirl all around.

So if you see us, don't turn away,
Join in the fun, come out and play!
For when stars are alight in the mischievous night,
We'll conquer the chaos with pure delight!

Swayed by Celestial Forces

Caught in the sway of the night's gentle pull,
I stumbled and tumbled, how wonderful!
With laughter as my partner, I leap and I twirl,
Dancing with candor, my heart in a whirl.

The stars are my friends, they giggle above,
With each whimsical twirl, I'm feeling their love.
I moonwalk in circles, giggles collide,
As the universe chuckles, I dance with pride.

Though gravity's tugging, I float on a dream,
Adventures await, or so it would seem.
I sway with the planets, oh what a delight,
In this whimsical waltz under beams shining bright.

So come join the frolic, lose track of your cares,
With joy in our hearts, we'll dance 'til it's rare.
In the rapture of night, let laughter soar high,
Swayed by forces of fun, we'll touch the sky!

Pull of the Celestial Tide

When the night is bright and round,
I dance like a fool on the ground.
The stars chuckle as I twirl,
Suggesting I give fate a whirl.

My neighbor's cat gives me a stare,
As I try to juggle and hair-dare.
They say it's the glint in my eye,
But it's just the shine in the sky.

I blame the sky for my antics bold,
And stories of mischief that need to be told.
I tripped on a shoe, fell flat on my face,
The universe rolled in a cosmic embrace.

With laughter echoing around the street,
I wonder who else will dance on their feet.
Under the night, I'm high on delight,
But it's the glimmering heavens that spark my flight.

Reflections of a Midnight Muse

At midnight, I plot with a grin,
When chaos is where my dreams begin.
A snack in hand, I leap with glee,
In the kitchen, the stars watch me.

I tried to bake a cake of the night,
But the frosting seemed to take a flight.
With sprinkles flying, oh what a scene,
That whisk had more moves than a dancing queen.

The clock strikes one, I'm still awake,
The neighbors sigh, "For goodness' sake!"
I blame the glimmer outside my door,
For every spill, and every uproar.

With laughter spilling into the air,
I'm simply a vessel, unaware.
The night hums songs of the jest I weave,
Where each giggle births what I believe.

Starlit Reckonings

Dusk brings ideas that simply can't wait,
With mischief and laughter, I seal my fate.
The twinkling lights whisper, "Go on, take a chance,"
While I're preparing for a wild moonlit dance.

On the rooftop, I feel like a star,
In a costume made from my pajamas far,
To the rhythm of crickets, I leap and I sway,
With aliens watching, I shout, "What a play!"

I spilled my drink on my shimmery shirt,
But all's fair in love and a bit of dessert.
My dog howls along as I spin and I glide,
The universe chuckles, I take it in stride.

Under the night sky, my heart's on the run,
With laughter and jests, I'm not yet done.
With starlit reckonings, I won't heed the morn,
For the antics of night are dear and reborn.

Shadows in the Moonlight

When darkness swells in a silver hue,
I find all my quirks are suddenly true.
With shadows that dance like silly old friends,
I invite the weirdness that nature sends.

A tree gave me shade and a vine gave a tease,
I laughed so loud; it brought me to my knees.
With twirls and giggles on this moonlit spree,
I was sure that even the shadows could see.

Not a whisper, just a comedic charade,
As I fought with my slippers, and nearly strayed.
A tumble, a chuckle, spills everywhere,
Those giggling shadows just don't seem to care.

In the depths of the night, we share this sweet thrill,
The moonlight and I plotting fun and ill will.
With each chuckle, I grow more bold, you see,
Blame it on twilight and its wizardry!

Stolen Moments by Lunar Light

In the dark where shadows prance,
I took a leap, a daring dance.
Socks unmatched, I twirl about,
The neighbors watch, they laugh and shout.

Glowing silver on my face,
I juggle snacks in silly grace.
A raccoon cheers from yonder tree,
With antics wild, it's just me free.

Forgot my keys, oh what a plight!
Blame it on that cheeky light.
A mischievous glint in the eve,
I swear it's got tricks up its sleeve!

As laughter bubbles in the night,
I chase my dreams till morning light.
With giggles caught in silvery beams,
I guess that's how it all seems.

Celestial Reckonings

Underneath the twinkling sphere,
I lost my mind and found some cheer.
A dance-off with a friendly cat,
Spinning around in my funny hat.

The rules of gravity took a break,
As I decided to bake a cake.
Flour flying, eggs in flight,
I laughed so hard, oh what a sight!

Each splash and splatter, a giggly sound,
Banana peels strewn on the ground.
It's simply a wild kind of night,
Where silly deeds feel just so right.

With moonbeams laughing from above,
I toast to life, to laughter, to love.
Best nights are those without a clue,
Just me, the stars, and a dance or two!

Reflections of a Blue-Hued Muse

I gazed into a silver lake,
Saw a frog with dreams to make.
In a crown of lilies, he sat proud,
With plans to leap, he sang out loud.

Mischief whispers in the air,
I tiptoe soft, to find some flair.
A picnic stolen at the moon's behest,
With sandwiches stuffed in my Sunday best.

A firefly likes to steal the show,
As I try to catch it, moving slow.
Yet tangled in my laughter's snare,
I trip and fall, with flair to spare!

With giggles echoing in the night,
The world feels warm and oh so bright.
So here's to jest and comic views,
In blue-hued nights and playful hues!

A Fable of the Night Sky

Once there lived a sly old fox,
Who danced upon the wooden blocks.
With twinkling eyes and a sneaky grin,
He whispered secrets to the wind.

In the glow of the starry night,
He twirled and spun, what a sight!
With every laugh, the stars aligned,
Creating mischief quite refined.

He borrowed cheese from a nearby store,
Then giggled loud, wanting more.
The moon gave chase, it had its fun,
While I rolled 'round, till the night was done.

Now tales are told of that cheeky fellow,
Who winks at life in shades of yellow.
So dance away, let laughter ring,
For whimsy lives in everything!

Pilgrimage to the Distant Hearth

In a silly dance, I prance away,
Chasing shadows that love to play.
With every step, my feet do twirl,
Spinning dreams in a wobbly whirl.

Stars are giggling in the night sky,
As I trip over my own shoe ties.
A glowing orb whispers secret tunes,
Urging me to howl with the raccoon goons.

Mischievous winds lift my silly hat,
While fireflies laugh, 'Now isn't that flat?'
My heart's a kite, soaring so high,
Crafting mischief as I pass by.

Home is but a wobbly line,
Yet each stumble feels so divine.
A pilgrimage of laughter and cheer,
To a hearth where silliness is clear.

Midnight Reveries of the Starry Canvas

Late at night with a wink and a grin,
I barter with stars, knowing I'll win.
They flicker back in a playful jest,
As my mind spins wild, ignoring the rest.

I draw constellations with my toes,
As laughter erupts from a nearby rose.
The sky winks knowingly, full of glee,
Encouraging nonsense, just like me!

With a nod to the owl, I make my case,
That juggling fireflies is a noble chase.
They flutter and giggle, my antics applaud,
While the night chuckles, as I dance unflawed.

In this gallery of dreams so bright,
Even chaos feels wonderfully right.
Midnight revels, a grand affair,
With each silly thought floating in the air.

Wandering Echoes of the Night's Pulse

Through the shadows, I skip and hop,
Each echo giggles, 'Don't ever stop!'
In this lively game, I lose my way,
As owls wink excitedly to play.

My shadow stretches, it strikes a pose,
As if to say, 'What do you suppose?'
With every bounce on this moonlit floor,
I hear the night whisper, 'Dance some more!'

Tickling the breezes, I leap with zeal,
My heart a drum, and oh, what a feel!
While crickets join with their sharp refrain,
In this wacky tune, I lose all my pain.

So round and round, like a rolling ball,
With laughter echoing, I feel so tall.
The night plays tricks, but I've found my bliss,
In these wandering echoes, I cannot miss.

Candles of the Night's Architecture

In the dark, I build with light,
Candles flicker, oh, what a sight!
Their dance creates a whimsical scene,
A feast of shadows, vibrant and keen.

With wobbly towers and dreams of wax,
I laugh as I put on my goofiest acts.
The night sways gently to my little song,
As I create chaos, where I belong.

A castle of giggles rises and falls,
With walls of humor and laughter in halls.
Every flicker shares a silly quip,
As I let my imagination zip.

So join me now, in this goofy spree,
Where candles laugh and the shadows flee.
In this architecture built from glee,
I find my joy, wild and free.

When the Night Calls

When night descends, I start to roam,
A silly dance, away from home.
With twinkling stars and laughter bright,
I blame it all on this strange night.

A squirrel chases me, what a sight,
I slip and slide, oh what a fright.
With gleeful giggles, I take a leap,
The shadows whisper, secrets to keep.

In the cool glow, I spin around,
Spilling ice cream on the ground.
The night just grins, my partner in crime,
Stirring mischief with every chime.

Oh, to be wild, with friends galore,
Crafting tales from the night before.
For when twilight comes to steal my heart,
I leap into joy, that's just the start!

Shadows Shift Under Celestial Watch

Under the gaze of sparkling lace,
I juggle apples, in such a race.
With shadows laughing, I strut my stuff,
Who knew nighttime could be so tough?

I trip on roots, and tumble down,
Grass stains now part of my frown.
Yet the glow overhead starts to tease,
With a silly grin, I dance with ease.

A raccoon joins in, what a crowd!
Dancing silly, feeling proud.
Under soft light, mischief will play,
Swaying with shadows, they lead the way.

Nighttime revels, what a surprise,
Finding giggles beneath dark skies.
With every slip and grin so wide,
The secret's safe, I must confide.

Embraced by Celestial Influences

The stars are winks, the clouds a laugh,
I set off on an epic path.
Moonbeams giggle as I sway,
Finding trouble in a fun way.

I tried to dance but bumped a tree,
The bark shouts back, 'What's wrong with thee?'
But with a wink, I'm back on my feet,
Twisting and turning, can't admit defeat.

The night's my friend, a trusty guide,
Echoing laughter wide and side.
I chase my shadow, it runs and hides,
With every launch, my heart collides.

Laughter lingers in soft air.
I'm lost in joy, without a care.
With starry friends, I gleefully shout,
Thanks to the guide, there's never a doubt.

Veiled Whispers

Whispers venture through the trees,
Carried softly on the breeze.
I dance beneath the hidden veil,
With each laugh, I leave a trail.

A cat appears, with sly intent,
It joins my path, my merriment.
Sneaky shadows, too close they creep,
Hilarity rises, no time for sleep.

Giggling winds sway the night,
In jestful rhythm, so light, so bright.
Can't tell what's dance or what's a sleep,
But all is merry, laughter's deep.

Spinning tales in the silver glow,
Secrets shared, just us and the show.
With every snap, a moment captured,
Funny fables, forever raptured.

Lunar Secrets

Secrets blossom in the night air,
Teasing smiles, daring flair.
Underneath the shady trees,
I twirl and chase, with giggles and wheezes.

An owl hoots, 'What's all this fuss?'
My blanket fort, it's made of dust!
But with laughter abundant, I will confess,
There's joy in chaos, I couldn't care less.

A curious fox joins the parade,
In our whimsical dance, it is unafraid.
With twinkling stars overhead,
I hop in circles, feel mischief spread.

Under the cover of a playful night,
Every movement feels just right.
For beneath the gaze of the luminous glow,
The secrets of laughter they forever bestow.

Secrets Behind the Glowing Veil

At night I toss and turn, in bed,
My thoughts are buzzing, dance in my head.
Whispers from shadows, they start to sing,
Behind every blanket, secrets take wing.

I giggle and snicker at the odd shadows,
Society's norms? I shall oppose!
A caper with critters, I swear makes sense,
In playful whispers, we build our defense.

Why limit the fun to the sun's bright face?
Night's giggling gossip will leave a trace.
With each tickle of the breeze from the side,
A cheerful hullabaloo I can't abide.

So if you catch me doing a jig,
It's just the night, making me big!
In laughter, I find a glowing delight,
A sparkle of mischief in every night.

Cravings of the Night-Blooming Heart

Under the stars, I wander in glee,
Craving the antics that won't let me be.
Dancing with shadows, my feet feel so light,
How silly it seems, but I just feel bright.

Nibbles of moonbeams are calling my name,
With every sneak bite, I feel more the same.
I chase at the giggles, the flickers of light,
A banquet of folly, a succulent sight.

My heart's a strange garden, with blooms full of cheer,
Each petal a laugh that my neighbors can hear.
Pies made of stardust, oh what a treat!
I relish the pranks and the night tastes sweet!

In the hush of the dark, let folly take flight,
With cravings for joy that ignite the night.
For who needs a reason to dance and to dream?
Everything's funny, or so it may seem.

Fantasia Under Luminous Clouds

In a world where giggles dare to float,
Luminous clouds, my whimsical boat.
I set sail on laughter, my heart takes flight,
As fantasies leap in the arms of the night.

A nerf dart or two launched with a cheer,
Who'd guess that mischief could endear?
With pillows as cushions and snacks all around,
The laughter grows louder in this crazy sound.

I swing from the branches of joy and jest,
Every twinkling moment, a quirky quest.
Artists at heart, we paint in pure glee,
In a landscape of chuckles, we're bound to be free.

Beneath all the cotton-candy skies,
Mirth hides in shadows, a sweet surprise.
The tales we spin, oh what a delight,
As we dance with the sprites in the glowing night.

Wandering Spirits in Night's Keep

Oh, mischievous spirits, where do you dwell?
In shadows and laughter, I know them so well.
They tug on my sleeves, and they dance through the air,
Their giggles and whispers lead me to dare.

With each little bump in the dark-cushioned night,
I journey with nonsense, a comical sight.
A jester in tow, we spin and we twirl,
In this raucous parade, my heart starts to swirl.

So if you see me in a fit of pure glee,
Join in the laughter, it's wild and free!
The tricks of the night, they're my trusted guides,
As I frolic with whimsy where laughter abides.

No secrets to keep, just joy to explore,
Wandering spirits, oh, what fun is in store!
Together we'll prance beneath stars all aglow,
In this funny realm where the silliness flows.

www.ingramcontent.com/pod-product-compliance
Lightning Source LLC
Chambersburg PA
CBHW071852160426
43209CB00003B/525